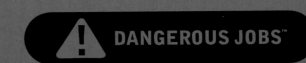
DANGEROUS JOBS™

STUNT PERFORMERS
AND STUNT DOUBLES

COPY 2

Lissette Gonzalez

PowerKiDS
press
New York

Published in 2008 by The Rosen Publishing Group, Inc.
29 East 21st Street, New York, NY 10010

First Edition

Editor: Jennifer Way
Book Design: Greg Tucker
Photo Researcher: Nicole Pristash

Photo Credits: Cover, pp. 5, 7, 15 © Shutterstock.com; pp. 9, 11, 13 © Getty Images; pp. 17, 19 © AFP/Getty Images; p. 21 © Getty Images Europe.

Library of Congress Cataloging-in-Publication Data

Gonzalez, Lissette, 1968–
  Stunt performers and stunt doubles / Lissette Gonzalez.
      p. cm. — (Dangerous jobs)
  Includes index.
  ISBN-13: 978-1-4042-3780-3 (library binding)
  ISBN-10: 1-4042-3780-1 (library binding)
  1. Stunt performers—Juvenile literature. I. Title.
  PN1995.9.S7G66 2008
  791.4302'8—dc22

                                        2006101532

Manufactured in the United States of America

CONTENTS

WHAT ARE STUNT PERFORMERS?

Stunt performers are people who do dangerous tricks. These tricks take special training to do safely. Stunt performers may jump over large objects on motorcycles or **parachute** from high up. They may stay underwater for a long time or even set themselves on fire. Stunt performers may also work as stunt doubles.

Some stunt performers do stunts in front of crowds and try to break records for different kinds of feats. Their stunts may be shown on TV. Other stunt performers work in movies. They are called stunt doubles. Stunt doubles take the place of actors in dangerous movie scenes.

Stunt performers get to learn cool skills, such as how to parachute from an airplane. It takes training to learn safe ways to do many of these kinds of tricks.

5

LEARNING STUNT SKILLS

People who do stunt work often say that they enjoyed **challenging** their bodies from an early age. Many stunt performers were gymnasts, martial artists, skateboarders, snowboarders, or mountain bikers as kids. These are all dangerous sports that take a lot of **physical** skill to do. As they grew up, these kids learned more and harder skills.

By practicing their skills, stunt performers get better at what they do. Practice also lowers the chance of getting hurt. They are so skilled at using their bodies that stunt performers are compared to top **athletes**.

This person is doing a freestyle motorcycle trick. Motorcycle stunt performers might go on to work in movies that have motorcycle chases or crashes in them.

STUNTS IN MOVIES

Like stunt performers, many stunt doubles are people who were athletic from a young age. Some stunt doubles may have done some acting before getting into stunt work. Other stunt doubles become actors or directors after they have done stunt work.

Jackie Chan is an actor who began his work as a stunt double and martial artist before starring in his own action movies. One of his first jobs as a stuntman was in the Bruce Lee movie *Enter the Dragon*. Chan has appeared in many movies and shows, including *Rush Hour*.

8

Jackie Chan is famous for doing his own stunts. Even though he tries to do stunts carefully, Chan has broken many bones while making his movies.

9

STUNT DOUBLES

Stunt doubles take the place of movie stars when a scene in a movie calls for their special skills. This is because most movie actors are not trained to use their bodies the way stunt doubles do. Although they are on-screen only for seconds, stunt doubles are actors, too. They have to perform their scenes so that audiences believe they are the star they are taking the place of.

Wayne Michaels is a stuntman known for performing high jumps. In the movie *GoldenEye*, Michaels **bungee jumped** from nearly 800 feet (244 m) up. The bungee sprung him back up nearly 200 feet (61 m)!

10

The stunt double in the Spider-Man suit takes the place of star Tobey Maguire for one of the many stunts in the movie *Spider-Man*.

11

PHYSICAL STUNTS

People who **specialize** in physical stunts are skilled in things like fighting, falling, **tumbling**, and leaping from high places. In some stunts they may also use **props**, like motorcycles or special ropes called harnesses. Physical stunt performers train for months or years to learn how to do a new stunt. Knowing how to fall safely is also helpful in case something goes wrong during a stunt.

Stunt performers often take gymnastics classes to prepare for their jobs. This kind of training is said to give a person "air sense." Air sense helps a person control his or her body during a tumble, flip, or fall.

This woman is bungee jumping. Bungee jumping can help give a person air sense.

13

DRIVING STUNTS

Some stunt performers go to stunt school. At stunt school, they get the chance to learn from people who have lots of stunt **experience**. Many stunt schools teach only driving stunts. Students learn tricks, like the high-speed slalom. For this trick, the driver moves from left to right to left while driving fast.

Stunt drivers may also learn how to drive backward, how to perform high-speed chases, or how to do donut turns. In a donut turn, the back of a car will make a large circle while the front makes a smaller circle. The tires leave marks on the ground that look like a donut.

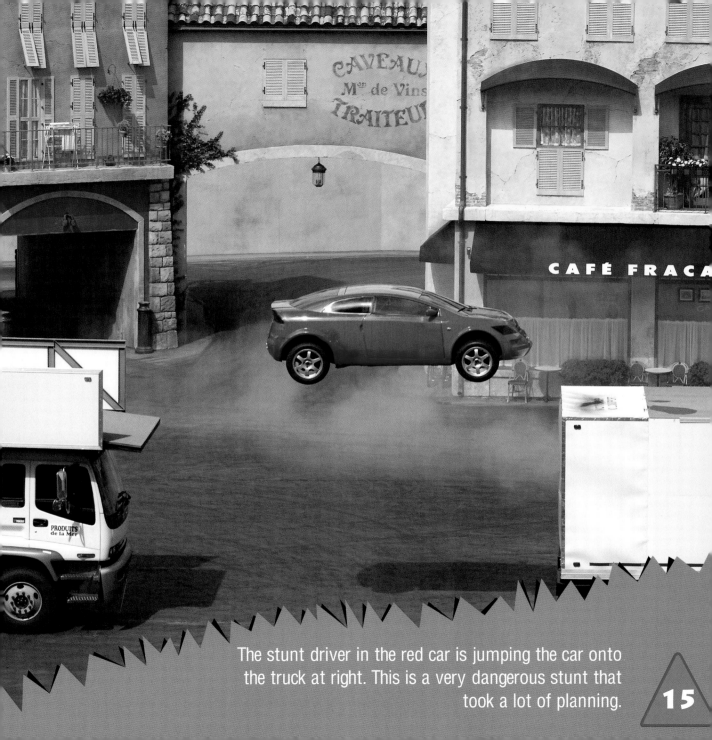

The stunt driver in the red car is jumping the car onto the truck at right. This is a very dangerous stunt that took a lot of planning.

15

FIRE STUNTS

Some stunt performers specialize in working with fire. Action movies often feature stunts with fire. Other fire stunts are fire breathing and fire eating. Fire-breathers spray gasoline into a flame and blow on it. It looks like a fireball is coming out of their mouths. Fire-eaters put flames into their mouths. The flames go out in their mouths, but it looks like they are eating the flame.

Fire stunt performers have to be careful to handle fire safely. They might use **flame retardants** to keep fire from spreading. They may also coat their clothes with a special **chemical** to keep from getting burned.

During fire stunts, like the one shown here, it is important that water and fire extinguishers are ready to be put to use.

17

STUNT COORDINATORS

People can get hurt doing stunts. Because of this, it is very important to plan stunts carefully. People who plan stunts are called stunt coordinators. Stunt coordinators talk about how the stunt will be performed and help the performers prepare. They let everyone who will take part in the stunt know what they must do. They also talk about the dangers.

Before the stunt happens, stunt coordinators check all the **equipment** to make sure it works. Safety equipment may be air bags to stop a fall, fire suits to keep a person from burning, or helmets to keep people safe in car crashes.

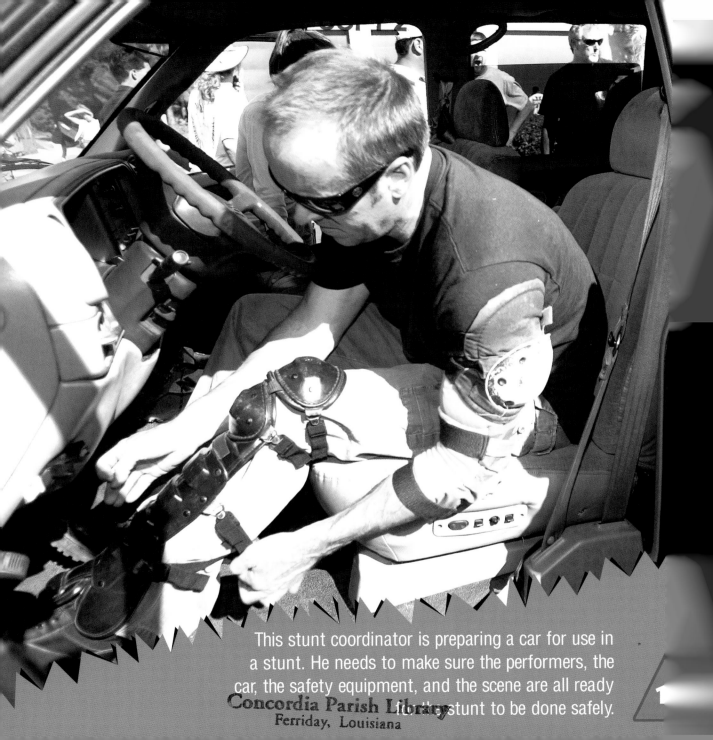

This stunt coordinator is preparing a car for use in a stunt. He needs to make sure the performers, the car, the safety equipment, and the scene are all ready for the stunt to be done safely.

DANGER ON THE SET

In 1982, a stunt went wrong and killed three people working on *Twilight Zone: the Movie*. After that, the movie and TV **industries** formed a safety committee, or group. The committee's job is to ensure the safety of stunt people. The U.S. government also has rules that people in stunt work must follow.

Even when stunt people follow the rules, things can go wrong. Fires can get out of control and burn people. A cable can snap, or air bags may have holes. Even though most stunts do not end badly, stunt performers know that they may be hurt or killed when they go to work.

Performer David Blaine does stunts for crowds, rather than in movies. He takes many chances in the stunts he does.

21

A THRILLING LIFE

Some stunt performers enjoy the **thrill** of doing things others cannot do. They get a rush out of jumping from airplanes or driving at high speeds and doing fast, cool stunts. Stunt performers also enjoy their work because they meet lots of people. Some perform for hundreds of people at a time. Others show their skills in movies or on TV.

Stunt performers may have many fans. David Blaine, for example, is a famous stunt performer. David Blaine once stayed in a block of ice for over 61 hours! Even though it can be dangerous, the life of a stunt performer can also be a lot of fun.

22

GLOSSARY

athletes (ATH-leets) People who take part in sports.

bungee jumped (BUN-gee JUMPT) Jumped from a high place while tied to a special rope that stretches.

challenging (CHA-lenj-ing) Requiring extra effort.

chemical (KEH-mih-kul) Matter that can be mixed with other matter to cause changes.

equipment (uh-KWIP-mint) All the supplies needed to do something.

experience (ik-SPEER-ee-ents) Knowledge or skill gained by doing or seeing something.

flame retardants (FLAYM rih-TAHR-dents) Matter that keeps things from burning.

industries (IN-dus-treez) Businesses.

parachute (PAR-uh-shoot) To jump safely from an aircraft using a large piece of cloth shaped like an umbrella.

physical (FIH-zih-kul) Having to do with the body.

props (PROPS) Things that are used in movies and in plays.

specialize (SPEH-shuh-lyz) To do something very well.

thrill (THRIL) A feeling of pleasure.

tumbling (TUM-bling) Falling suddenly in a controlled way.

23

INDEX

WEB SITES

Due to the changing nature of Internet links, PowerKids Press has developed an online list of Web sites related to the subject of this book. This site is updated regularly. Please use this link to access the list:
www.powerkidslinks.com/djob/stunt/